Presented to

LeAnne
_____

On the occasion of

2L th Birthday
_____

From

Chris
_____

Date

1 - 23 - 01
_____

Published by Barbour Publishing, Inc., P. O. Box 719, Uhrichsville, Ohio 44683
http://www.barbourbooks.com

 Member of the
Evangelical Christian
Publishers Association

Printed in China.

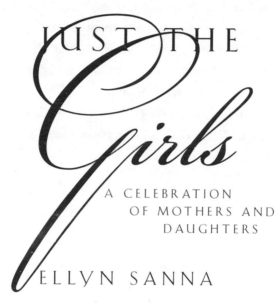

JUST THE Girls

A CELEBRATION OF MOTHERS AND DAUGHTERS

ELLYN SANNA

BARBOUR
PUBLISHING, INC.

$\mathcal{O}$ne of my earliest memories is of my mother singing "Jesus Loves You"—and from my mother's gentle hands I learned what love meant. Because her life taught me the meaning of this word, today I pass love on to my daughter; through me, she catches a glimpse of the God who loves her unconditionally and eternally.

I am grateful that God gave me a mother who loved me. And I am grateful for the daughter He has given me to love. I pray that He will be always revealed in our love for each other.

For this is the message that ye heard from the beginning,
that we should love one another.
1 JOHN 3:11, KJV

Your love for one another will prove to the world
that you are my disciples.
JOHN 13:35, NLT

Circles of Love

MOTHERS OF DAUGHTERS ARE DAUGHTERS
OF MOTHERS AND HAVE REMAINED SO,
IN CIRCLES JOINED TO CIRCLES,
SINCE TIME BEGAN.

SIGNE HAMMER

LINKED TO THE PAST,
TOUCHING THE FUTURE

*O*ne hot day last summer, my seventy-five-year-old mother, my eleven-year-old daughter, and I walked together across a sun-baked lawn. My mother's heart was bothering her, and we walked very slowly, but my daughter didn't mind; she's been complaining that I walk too fast ever since she was small. I listened to their soft voices, watching the way their heads bent toward each other, and I was startled to realize that my daughter is taller than my mother now. My mother said something and I heard my daughter laugh out loud with delight.

And at that moment, I was suddenly, completely happy. I didn't want to be anywhere but right there, with the young woman to whom I had given life, with the older woman who had given me life. I thought of another woman, my mother's mother, now in heaven, and I imagined a young woman who is yet to be born, my daughter's daughter. Together we form a chain, a chain of love reaching from the past into the future.

Family faces are magic mirrors.
Looking at people who belong to us,
we see the past, present and future.
GAIL LUMET BUCKLEY

HEIRLOOMS WE DON'T HAVE
IN OUR FAMILY.
BUT STORIES WE'VE GOT.
ROSE CHERNIN

The relationship between a mother and her daughter is as varied,
as mysterious, as constantly changing and interconnected
as the patterns that touch, move away from,
and touch again in a kaleidoscope.
LYN LIFSHIN

THE ART OF MOTHERING
IS HANDED DOWN
FROM ONE GENERATION TO THE NEXT.
WENDY JEAN RUHL

It seems but yesterday you lay new in my arms. . . .
Years slip away—today we are mothers together.
RUTH GRAHAM BELL,
Mothers Together

WOMEN PASS ON FROM MOTHER
TO DAUGHTER. . .AT AN EVERYDAY LEVEL
OF PRACTICAL CARING AND
AT A DEEPER LEVEL. . . . THIS LEGACY
IS A TEACHER OF LOVE—THE FIRST TEACHER
AND THE MOST IMPORTANT. . . .

RACHEL BILLINGTON

*I see generations of women bearing a flame. . .handing it down
from one to another, burning. It is a gift of fire, transported from
a world far off and far away, but never extinguished. And now,
in this very moment, my mother imparts the care of it to me.
I must keep it alive. . . . I must hand it on
when the time comes to my daughter.*

KIM CHERNIN

May she have daughters of her own
to care when she is old and I am gone.
RUTH GRAHAM BELL,
Mothers Together

Lessons We Learn from Each Other

THE OLDER WOMEN. . .CAN TRAIN
THE YOUNGER WOMEN TO LOVE THEIR
HUSBANDS AND CHILDREN, TO BE
SELF-CONTROLLED AND PURE,
TO BE BUSY AT HOME, TO BE KIND. . . .

TITUS 2:3–5, NIV

*I*f my mother had been a different woman, I would be a different person. When she read to me each night, I learned about the world of words; today I make my living writing—and I still love coming home from the library with a stack of books to keep me company. When my mother took me outdoors and named the trees and flowers and birds for me, I learned about the world of nature; today, whenever I'm upset or discouraged, I still find peace walking in the woods, and when I recognize ash and beech, trilliums and hepatic, purple finches and indigo buntings, I feel as though I'm saying the names of dear, old friends. And when my mother prayed with me each night and before each meal, I learned about an eternal world; today I seek God's presence daily and offer up my life to Him in prayer.

My mother trained me well.

Teach your children to choose the right path,
and when they are older, they will remain upon it.
PROVERBS 22:6, NLT

There is no influence so powerful as that of the mother.
SARAH JOSEPHA HALE (1788–1879)

WHEN I STOPPED SEEING MYSELF
WITH THE EYES OF A CHILD,
I SAW THE WOMAN
WHO HAD HELPED ME
GIVE BIRTH TO MYSELF.
NANCY FRIDAY

There is so much to teach, and the time goes by so fast.
ERMA BOMBECK

*O*h, no, it's raining again!" My three-year-old hand flew to my forehead.

"Yes, Miss Drama." My mother smiled and shook her head. "I should have named you Greta, after a famous actress."

Somehow, the name stuck; Greta became one of my mother's favorite names for me.

Occasionally, though, I did hear my given name. On those occasions, my mother accented each syllable: "Don-na I-rene!" I'd always cringe when I heard both my first and middle names; I knew whatever my mother wanted to say to me, it was serious. Thankfully, those times were few and far between.

When I was a small child, my mother was simply "Mommy," nothing more and nothing less. As I grew older, though, her name changed to "Mom." Then one night at dinner I nicknamed her.

"Gracias, Madre," I said as she filled my bowl with her homemade chili.

She laughed. "Must be you're learning something in Spanish class."

From then on, we used our choice names for each other. I left telephone messages on the kitchen counter labeled, "For Madre." When I went to college, my mailbox contained letters addressed to Greta.

And then one day, out of the blue, my mother changed her name again. I still remember the phone call.

"Donna," she began, "I've regressed twenty-five years. From now on you might as well call me Helen."

What could she have done? I had never called her by her given name. Maybe she had dyed her hair jet black. I couldn't believe she would have done anything truly scandalous. I took a deep breath. "What did you do?"

She hesitated, then blurted, "I had my ears pierced."

I burst into laughter, and we giggled together like teenagers while she related her trip to the mall with my aunt. Mother's purchases? A hole in each earlobe and a pair of fourteen-karat gold posts.

My next visit home I handed her a gift. "Helen, this is to honor your new youthful image," I told her.

After she opened the small box, she stood in front of the mirror. Carefully, she poked in the earrings I'd bought her, then stepped back to admire the white feathers that dangled from gold hoops.

"I figured white would go with everything," I said.

Every time she wore those earrings, I swelled with pride and joy. I felt the same way years ago when she wore my handmade macaroni necklaces.

I'm grown up now, but I still don't call my mother Helen—it's either Madre or Mom. Friends use first names, but my relationship with my mother is much more than merely friendship. But I always feel special when she calls me Greta; the love and acceptance expressed by that choice name give me a glimpse of the eternal identity God has lovingly created for me.

And I can imagine the following scene when I go to heaven:

"God, where is my mother? You know—Helen. She's probably wearing white feather earrings."

"Oh, you mean Madre?"

"Yes!"

"She's right here waiting for you, Greta."

DONNA LANGE

In the eyes of its mother every beetle is a gazelle.
AFRICAN PROVERB

NO MATTER HOW PERFECT
YOUR MOTHER THINKS YOU ARE,
SHE WILL ALWAYS WANT TO
FIX YOUR HAIR.
SUZANNE BEILENSON

What do girls do who haven't any mothers
to help them through their troubles?
LOUISA MAY ALCOTT

AS DAUGHTERS, WHEN WE SHARE
OUR HEARTS WITH OUR MOTHERS,
WE CAN LEARN FROM
THEIR EXPERIENCE. . .

My Dear Mary,

How lonely the house seems—I never knew before how you helped to fill it. I am anxious to hear of your first impressions of. . .your new home. Ever since you went away, I have been wondering if it was as hard for you to go out into the world as it was for me to have you go.

Don't write short, hurried letters, simply stating facts in their tersest form, but tell me all your thoughts and dreams and plans, your worries and trials, and we will talk them over as two comrades. . . . If there is anything in my life that can be of value to you, I want you to have it; if I can save you a stumble or a single false step, I want to do it, but the only way I can do it is to know your heart.

Your loving mother.

FLORENCE WENDEROTH SAUNDERS (1908)

NO MATTER HOW OLD WE ARE,
WE STILL CONTINUE TO LEARN
FROM OUR MOTHERS. . .

*W*henever I feel myself inferior to everything about me. . . , I can still hold up my head and say to myself: "I am the daughter of the woman who. . .at the age of seventy-six was planning journeys and undertaking them. . . . I am the daughter of a woman who, in a mean, close-fisted, confined little place, opened her village house to stray cats, tramps and pregnant servant-girls. I am the daughter of a woman who many times, when she was in despair at not having enough money for others, ran through the wind-whipped snow to cry from door to door, at the houses of the rich, that a child had just been born in a poverty-stricken home to parents whose feeble, empty hands had no swaddling clothes for it. Let me not forget that I am the daughter of a woman who bent her head, trembling, between the blades of a cactus, her wrinkled face full of ecstasy over the promise of a flower, a woman who herself never ceased to flower, untiringly, during three quarters of a century.

COLETTE

$\mathcal{W}$e not only learn from our mothers, though. As a mother, I learn something new from my daughters almost every day.

The moment my oldest daughter was born, I was awestruck that God could have loved me so much that He would entrust into my care this perfect, beautiful little person. And as she grew older, I learned to play again, to laugh out loud at silly things. I learned that children's books are as good as grown-up volumes, and I learned that playing in the creek is still as much fun as it was when I was small. When I did the laundry, my daughter would stand on a chair beside me, watching the swirling clothes in the washing machine, and I learned that even ordinary chores are full of joy.

As I write this I look out my window and see my daughter walking toward me, home from school. She's no longer very excited about the laundry—but as she comes through the door, her smile delights me as much as it did when I would pick her up out of her crib after a nap. And the love she gives me, the daily forgiveness she grants me when I'm impatient, the understanding she extends when I'm discouraged, all these things teach me that God's love for me is still both awesome and full of joy.

MY DAUGHTER INTRODUCED ME TO THE
SOOTHING LUXURY OF A BUBBLE BATH AND
TO THE CHARMS OF READING OUT LOUD
AND PRETENDING. HER EXPRESSIVENESS
HAS ENCOURAGED MY OWN.
I FIND THE EDGES OF MY PERSONALITY
ROUNDING OUT. . . .
ANGELA MCBRIDE

In sharing your childhood discoveries,
I have relived my own.
MARION C. GARRETTY

THE THING ABOUT MOTHERS IS. . .

You can't lie when you're looking into their eyes.

When they're on a diet, everyone in the family has to be on a diet, too.

All their daughters are geniuses.

They are each and every one the best cook in the entire world.

They always take your side in an argument—unless you're arguing with them.

No matter how old you get, they're the best people to have around when you are sick.

THE THING ABOUT DAUGHTERS IS. . .

Even when they're not with you, you can never escape their presence in your heart.

They need love the most when they are hardest to love.

Once they're teenagers, no matter how much they love you, they're still embarrassed by you.

They are so much like you, and yet so different.

They break your heart one moment and make you laugh with joy the next.

They often steal your clothes from your closet and yet will never listen to your advice when the two of you shop for clothes.

Letting Go

A MOTHER IS NOT A PERSON TO
LEAN ON BUT A PERSON
TO MAKE LEANING UNNECESSARY.

DOROTHY CANFIELD FISHER (1879–1958)

As daughters, it's hard to let go of our mothers. No matter how old we are, we still hear their voices in our heads. But as much as we love them, as much as they love us, God wants His voice to be louder than our mothers'.

As mothers, it's hard to let go of our daughters. We would like to be with them wherever they go in life, protecting them from all life's dangers. But God wants us to put our daughters in His hands, trusting that His love will provide for them far better than we ever could.

I love my daughter. She and I have shared my body.
There is a part of her mind that is part of mine.
But when she was born, she sprang from me like a slippery fish,
and has been swimming away ever since.

AMY TAN

IT'S LIKE A MAGNET,
THE MOTHER-DAUGHTER RELATIONSHIP.
ONE DAY, YOUR DAUGHTER
CLINGS FOR DEAR LIFE;
THE NEXT, SHE'S PUSHING YOU AWAY.

KAREN PHILLIPS

[My] girls aren't something I created; I feel like I received the honor
of being the vehicle for bringing these souls into the world. . . .
But I don't make the mistake of thinking I own them.

ROSANNE CASH

SOMETIMES THE BEST WAY TO LET GO IS BY FORGIVING. . .

*M*y first-grade daughter is still convinced I'm the most beautiful woman in the world. But a few mornings ago my sixth-grader was embarrassed by my appearance.

She was already around the corner, waiting for the school bus, when I noticed her lunch bag sitting on the kitchen table. Without thinking twice, I grabbed it up, and dressed in my sweats, my hair still rumpled from my pillow, I dashed down the sidewalk, my old moccasins slipping and sliding on my feet. "Emily!" I shouted. "You forgot your lunch."

She threw a horrified look at me, and her eyes filled with tears. The other kids waiting for the bus whispered and giggled to each other. I glanced from them to my daughter, and suddenly I realized that I hardly looked my best. And I remembered once more what it felt like to be that age, when each small discrepancy in a person's appearance was fair game for ridicule and laughter.

Who cares? I wanted to tell her. Don't let yourself be as petty as they are. Do you think I care what a bunch of twelve-year-olds thinks of me?

But I cared what she thought of me. And it hurt to know that for the first time in her life, she was ashamed of me.

That day after school, she and I were especially nice to each other. I knew she had forgiven me for embarrassing her. And I forgave her for no longer thinking I was the most beautiful and perfect woman in the world. I guess I was really forgiving her for growing up.

RAISING DAUGHTERS IS
LIKE MOUNTAIN CLIMBING. . .
YOU CAN'T KEEP THEM FROM
TAKING CHANCES IN LIFE.
THEY'RE GOING TO LEAVE
NO MATTER WHAT—IT'S MAKING SURE
YOU'VE USED THE RIGHT ROPE AND GIVEN
THE RIGHT AMOUNT OF SLACK.

EILEEN BROWN

*One of the most valuable lessons I learned. . .is that we all
have to learn from our mistakes and we learn from those mistakes
a lot more than we learn from the things we succeeded in doing.
I have to give my. . .daughters the opportunity to make mistakes.*

ANN RICHARDS

I LOOKED AT THIS ROLLED-UP BUNDLE. . .
AND KNEW AGAIN
I HAD NOT CREATED HER.
SHE WAS HERSELF APART FROM ME.
SHE HAD HER OWN LIFE TO LEAD,
HER OWN DESTINY TO ACCOMPLISH;
SHE JUST CAME PAST ME TO THIS EARTH.
MY JOB WAS TO GET HER TO ADULTHOOD
AND PUSH HER OFF.

KATHARINE TREVELYAN

*Our goal is to steadily turn our [daughters] away from
their earthly parents, who will let them down,
toward a heavenly Father who will always be there for them
and in whose arms they will always be secure.*

SUSAN ALEXANDER YATES

Hearts
Entwined
Forever

YOUR RELATIONSHIP WITH YOUR
DAUGHTERS IS ONE YOU CAN RELY ON,
THERE FOR LIFE, AN ONGOING,
DEVELOPING RELATIONSHIP.

ENID JOHNS

*W*hen my daughter Emily was little, she was my constant companion. Her little chattering voice brought new life to everything I did, from family visits to grocery shopping, from trips to the bank to walks in the woods. Once, waiting in an examination room for my doctor, the two of us were talking a blue streak when the nurse came in. "You two are best buddies, aren't you?" she said. And we were.

When Emily went to preschool for the first time, I gave her a gold heart of mine to wear, to remind her that my love went with her. When I went into the hospital for the birth of my second child, she gave it back to remind me that her love would be with me. And when she went to kindergarten, I bought her a duplicate necklace, so that she would know she was always in my heart.

But as she grew older and my life got busier, filled now with two more children and the responsibilities of my career, I sometimes worried that I would lose her, that she would disappear into her own new world of school and friends, and I would never recover the person who had been such a good companion to me.

But lately, as she becomes a young woman instead of a child, I find we relate to each other in a new way. Now, as we lie on my big bed and have woman-to-woman talks, I realize she's still a good companion. And yesterday, as she was hurrying off to meet her friends, I noticed the small gold heart that glittered at her throat. I touched the gold heart around my own neck and smiled.

The daughter never gives up on the mother,
just as the mother never gives up on the daughter.
There is a tie here so strong nothing can break it.
RACHEL BILLINGTON

IT'S MY BELIEF THAT BETWEEN MOTHERS
AND DAUGHTERS THERE IS A KIND
OF BLOOD-HYPHEN THAT IS,
FINALLY, INDISSOLUBLE.
CAROL SHIELDS

Once a mother, always a mother—even if your daughter is seventy.
The relationship changes, of course, but is no less important.
RACHEL BILLINGTON

A daughter and her mother are never free of another. . . .
For they are so entwined in heart and mind that. . .
they share each love, each joy,
each sorrow and each bitter wrong life-long.
PAM BROWN

A WOMAN SHOULD ALWAYS STAND
BY A WOMAN.
EURIPIDES

How vast a memory has Love!
ALEXANDER POPE

Looking Toward the Future

AND ALL THY CHILDREN SHALL BE
TAUGHT OF THE LORD;
AND GREAT SHALL BE THE PEACE
OF THY CHILDREN.

Isaiah 54:13, KJV

*M*y mother still worries about me. She longs for my happiness and well-being, and I suspect my illnesses are far harder on her than they are on me. I know her prayers go with me wherever I go.

As my own daughters grow up, I know that I, too, will worry about them until the day I die. I cannot protect them from all pain. But my prayer for them is that they will be strong in Christ Jesus, that in Him they will find their peace. He will still be with them when I am gone. And I can trust their growing-up years, their adulthood, their old age, and even their deaths to Him.

A kindhearted woman gains respect.
PROVERBS 11:16, NIV

SHE WORE AGE SO GRACEFULLY,
SO CARELESSLY, THAT THERE WAS A
SACRED BEAUTY ABOUT HER FADED CHEEK
MORE LOVELY AND LOVABLE THAN ALL
THE BLOOM OF HER YOUTH.
HAPPY WOMAN WHO WAS NOT AFRAID
OF GROWING OLD.
DINAH MARIA MULOCK

Your beauty. . .should be that of your inner self,
the unfading beauty of a gentle and quiet spirit,
which is of great worth in God's sight.
1 PETER 3:3–4, NIV

If you have made mistakes, even serious ones,
there is always another chance for you.
What we call failure is not the falling down,
but the staying down.
MARY PICKFORD

OUR DAUGHTERS ARE THE MOST PRECIOUS
OF OUR TREASURES, AND THE DEAREST
POSSESSIONS OF OUR HOMES,
AND THE OBJECTS OF OUR
MOST WATCHFUL LOVE.
MARGARET E. SANGSTER

Keep your face to the sunshine and you cannot see the shadow.
HELEN KELLER

Never grow a wishbone, daughter,
where your backbone ought to be.
CLEMENTINE PADDLEFORD

NO ONE CAN MAKE YOU FEEL INFERIOR
WITHOUT YOUR CONSENT.
ELEANOR ROOSEVELT

There is nothing Madison Avenue can give us
that will make us more beautiful women.
We are beautiful because God created us that way.
MARIANNE WILLIAMSON

FLOWERS GROW
OUT OF DARK MOMENTS.
CORITA KENT

Life is change.
Growth is optional.
Choose wisely.
KAREN KAISER

*T*hank You, God, for the gift of my mother. Bless her, please, with Your love and kindness. May she always walk with You.

And, God, thank You for my daughter. Care for her, watch over her, lead her in paths of truth. May she always know You are with her.

Thank You, Lord, for creating both of these wonderful women. I am so grateful for mothers and daughters!